THE HYMNS OF HERMES

G. R. S. Mead

THE HYMNS OF HERMES

G.R.S. MEAD

WITH AN INTRODUCTION BY
STEPHAN A. HOELLER

WEISERBOOKS
Boston, MA/York Beach, ME

This edition first published in 2006 by
Red Wheel/Weiser, LLC
York Beach, ME
With offices at:
368 Congress Street
Boston, MA 02210
www.redwheelweiser.com

Library of Congress Cataloging-in-Publication Data
available upon request from the Library of Congress

ISBN 1-57863-359-1

Printed in the USA
CM

13 12 11 10 09 08 07 06
 8 7 6 5 4 3 2 1

The paper used in this publication meets the minimum
requirements of the American National Standard for
Information Sciences—Permanence of Paper for Printed
Library Materials Z39.48-1992 (R1997).

CONTENTS

INTRODUCTION
Our Hermetic Heritage

Who Was Hermes?

Some religions, such as Buddhism, Christianity, Islam and Confucianism possess human founders; others, like Taoism, Shinto and Hinduism grew from early, probably Shamanistic beginnings to their later condition of sublime grandeur. Two religions represent an exception to both of these categories: Gnosticism and Hermeticism. There was no special person who founded Gnosticism, although the majority of Gnostic teachers came to attach themselves to the then brand new movement of Christianity, and most Gnostic scriptures make repeated and reverential references to Jesus. Similarly, there was no man by the name of Hermes who founded the 'religion of the Mind,' or as it became known: Hermeticism. The origins of the Hermetic teachings are lost in the land of myth and legend, which did not stop the Hermetic teachers from attaching their system to the name and figure of Hermes.

Hermes was the Greek god of the higher Mind, and so may be called a god, or even *the* God of Wisdom. Any writings within a particular time and within a certain cultural milieu that were held to be inspired by true Divine Wisdom were attributed to the God of Wisdom, and were frequently said to be written by Hermes himself. These were times wherein personal ambition and vainglory were considered to be incompatible with religious pursuits, and thus it appeared natural that various individual writers who considered themselves inspired by Wisdom would state that their books were written by Hermes. This use of a mythic pseudonym had most certainly no motive of deceit in it; such a practice was common in the literary genre of inspired spiritual literature. Customs of this sort persisted into much later periods. Thus we have no inkling of the true authorship of the *Zohar*. The quasi-author of this book, the fabled Rabbi Shimon ben Yochai, had little or no connection with the work. Even in the twentieth century, the mystical psychologist, C. G. Jung would not sign his own name to his poetic Gnostic treatise *Septem Sermones ad Mortuos*, but named Basilides of Alexandria as its author. Such acknowledgement of credit to where it spiritually belongs must be seen as a sign of commendable humility in any age!

Thus we must understand that the various writings which may be grouped under the heading of 'Hermetica,' are in the modern sense anonymous. By the same token we must also be cognizant of the possibility that they were all inspired by a certain mysterious spiritual principle, which in today's language might be described as an archetype, and to which the name Hermes was given.

The Hermes appearing in the literature of Hermeticism is not the Greek Hermes pure and simple. Rather, it is quite certain that this figure is closely connected with the Wisdom God of ancient Egypt, Thout or Tahuti. As far back as 5000 years ago there existed in Chmun, the 'City of the Eight,' or Hermopolis (as it came to be called in Greek), a great center of worship dedicated to this deific figure. He played part in the creation myth of Pharaonic Egypt; he was also the keeper and author of the records of the Gods, and a psychopomp, a guide of the souls in the underworld. He was regarded as the author of all writing and the actual scribe who wrote the ancient scriptures. He supervised the drawing up of the laws and saw to it that these and other holy books would be preserved in appropriate libraries. He was known as the Lord of the Moon who was in charge of the mysterious and dark world of the night. More than this, he was himself the Divine Word from which all the manifest worlds arose. (The Logos concept enunciated by Philo and utilized by Christianity may have been derived from the Egyptian God of Wisdom.) In the myth of Osiris and Isis he was the master-magician who taught Isis how to bring her slain royal spouse back to life and thus conceive the conquering savior, Horus.

It was to this awesome and inspiring God-image that the Greeks of the Hellenistic age joined their own God of Wisdom, Hermes, whose name became the normative apellation of the archetypal figure subsumed under this name.

Hermetic and Gnostic Communities

In the first volume of his greatest work on Hermetica, *Thrice-Greatest Hermes*, G. R. S. Mead presented a graphic account of the impressive religious enthusiasm and inventive enterprise of the Hellenistic age, and has demonstrated how great a role the figure of the Greco-Egyptian Hermes played in the spiritual flowering of the time. In his other important work, *Fragments of a Faith Forgotten*, he demonstrated that there were, in fact, two major related spiritual movements active within the period indicated: Hermeticism and Gnosticism. The two had much more in common than many writers assume, the principal difference between them being that the former utilized the figure of

Hermes as the archetype of salvific wisdom, while the latter had usually accepted the recently arisen Messianic figure of Jesus in a similar manner. Both Hermeticists and Gnostics used the term *Gnosis* to describe the experience of liberating interior knowledge; both regarded the physical world, or cosmos, as a place of confinement from whence Gnosis can liberate the human spirit. The affinity existing between the two schools is borne out by the fact that in the now increasingly famous Nag Hammadi library of the Egyptian Gnostics, several works of purely Hermetic character were found. It is very likely that Christian Gnostics and Pagan Hermeticists freely availed themselves of each other's literature and derived benefits therefrom.

It is quite likely that the members of the Hermetic communities were primarily Egyptian men and women, who having been brought up in the immemorial traditions of their land preferred an Egyptian archetypal structure to the Semitic one of Christian Gnosticism, or of Jewish Essenism, or even to the Greek orientation of Neoplatonic and Neopythagorean mysticism.

Like the Gnostics, these devotees of Hermes were no mere syncreticists, artificially combining Greek, Egyptian and other magico-philosophical elements to form a new system. As C. G. Jung said about the Gnostics, they worked with original, compelling images of the deep unconscious; they were men or women who experienced deep realizations and communed with powerful images in states of ecstasy and visionary transport. Their writings, as any reader can easily recognize, are full of beauty and poetic rhythm, replete with intense feeling generated by profound individual experience of the mysteries beyond physical existence.

Gnostics and Hermeticists both based their lives and work on the proposition that intimate, first-hand and personal knowledge of divine things is possible for human beings. Indeed, it may be said that they held that unless a human being enters into an intimate relationship with the Divine, his or her life has been lacking in anything that could be called true fulfilment. Many of these men and women pursued their high objectives by withdrawing from the superficialities of worldly life into the solitudes of the deserts, there to spend their lives in mystic exercises combined with fervent study. Others remained in the great cities, such as Alexandria, where they recruited new converts to their cause and combined honest lives in the world with the pursuit of things beyond the world.

We possess no names of writers and teachers of the Hermetic works, for the aforementioned reason that their books were said to have been written by Hermes himself. We know of no Hermetic master to be compared with the Gnostic masters, such as Valentinus, Basilides, Carpocrates and others. This should not lead us to believe, however, that great teachers and initiators did not exist in the Hermetic communities. The fascinating treatise in the Nag Hammadi collection, entitled *The Eighth Reveals the Ninth* (Nag Hammadi Codex VI, Tractate 6) describes the spiritual experiences of a Hermetic teacher (referred to as 'father') and of a student (called 'son') and gives us a charming picture of the spiritual relationship as it apparently existed between master and disciple in a Hermetic community. The anonymous seers and sages of the Hermetic movement were undoubtedly persons well worth knowing, individuals whose repeated experiences of an exalted form of consciousness qualified them as guides and facilitators of the Gnosis of those who came to them for initiatory instruction.

Hermetic Curriculum

The Hermetic method of instruction may be envisioned as having functioned along the following lines: [*]

[*] The writer of this Introduction is indebted for much of this scheme of Hermetic initiatory progress to Lewis S. Keizer's commentaries to Nag Hammadi Codex VI, Tractate 6. (*The Eighth Reveals the Ninth: A New Hermetic Initiation Discourse* [Seaside, CA: Academy of Arts and Humanities, 1974], 58–63.)

The first step undertaken by a Hermetic cat-echumen consisted in reading some of the publicly available Hermetic books, such as portions of the *Corpus Hermeticum* or the *Poimandres*, as well as in attending some public discourses given by a Hermetic teacher. The setting for such study and instruction would have been in open meetings and public places. This phase of the process would have been regarded as a period of probation.

The second period occurred in small groups com-posed of students who have passed their probation-ary period. Rituals and meditations were performed in this phase, many of these devoted to acquaint the student with the spiritual atmosphere of the exis-tential condition wherein he or she is present. The experiences undergone here were regarded as pre-paratory to the ascent through the seven spheres which was to occur at the next step. Crucial at this time was the aspirant's ability to differentiate himself or herself from the cosmos, and realize the spiritual identity residing at the center of the soul: an identity that is forever different from roles and false identi-ties foisted upon the person by the world.

Next came a process which Hermeticists shared with Gnostics and with the later-surfacing Kabbalists. It is known as the progress through the Hebdomad. The seven sacred planets of the ancient world were widely envisioned as the symbolic guardians of earthly life. Through their regions the soul descends into earthly manifestation and through them it must ascend again to freedom and light. The planets were largely regarded as influences of restriction, which the ascending soul must overcome. As the initiate's interior powers increase, the stranglehold of the cosmos and the planets decreases. (One may recall that many centuries later, the mysterious foundress of the Hermetic Order of the Golden Dawn, Frl. Anna Sprengel was known by the motto: "Sapiens dominabitur astris"—"the wise shall exercise dominion over the stars"—denoting an attitude not very common among astrologers.)

In this period of initiatory development, the Hermetic student was guided to such acquisition of mental and spiritual power that would enable him or her to cast off the chains of the cosmic jailers. Disciplines involving personal behavior, devotional activities and special topical discourses assisted the student in this work. The setting was that of a tutorial format, one pupil at the time.

Having overcome the seven spheres, and with them the limiting influence of the cosmos, the initiate was now ready to enter the 'Brotherhood of the Ogdoad.' This step is symbolized by the entry into the eighth sphere, beyond the cosmic prison-house of the seven. In this experience the Hermetic initiate becomes one with the deeper self resident in the soul and comes to recognize that infinite dimensions of further spiritual progress now await the transformed soul. This initiation is administered in a totally private setting in the context of a revelatory dialogue with an initiator, who appears as the embodiment of Hermes. The tone of this experience is quite ecstatic, that is, characterized by a very much altered consciousness.

In addition to, or possibly in conjunction with the aforementioned phases of initiatory progress, there were administered also what might be called Hermetic sacraments, in many ways similar to the esotericized Christian sacraments administered by the Gnostics, which are mentioned in *The Gospel of Philip*. In various portions of the *Corpus Hermeticum*, mention is made of a kind of anointing with "ambrosial water" and of a self-administered baptism in a basin, the *krater*, a mysterious container sent down from above by Hermes.

The Role of Hymns of Praise in Hermeticism

The last initiatory phase described above appears to be the one wherein the genre of spiritual poetry that has been described as a 'hymn' finds its most prominent place. Initiator and initiate alike undergo radically altered states of consciousness within this, the highest mystery liturgy. A natural need arising in such states is the utterance of statements describing one's exalted condition. Thus in the initiation discourse alluded to earlier, called *The Eighth Reveals the Ninth*, which is contained in the Nag Hammadi collection, we hear the initiator, ('father') utter the following descriptive ecstatic statement:

> How shall I describe this all? I see another mind that moves the soul. I see the one who speaks to me through a holy swoon. Thou givest me strength. I see myself! I am willing to discourse! I am overcome with trembling: I have found the origin of the Power above all powers, which has no origin: I see a well-spring bubbling up with life!
>
> I have said, O thou son, that I am the Mind. I have seen what speech cannot reveal, for the entire Eighth, O my son, with the souls therein and the angels are singing in silence. But I the Mind understand.

The essence of the Hermetic hymn seems to be that it represents a literary form wherein the ecstatic experience of the Hermetic initiate can find poetic expression. Altered states of consciousness seldom if ever lend themselves to prosaic, verbal-conceptual and exhortative treatment. On the contrary, only poetic, emotionally charged, imaginative language can even begin to do such experiences justice. Mead was indeed correct when he wrote that the singing of these kinds of hymns on earth is the reflection of a heavenly mystery. What needs to be emphasized is that this heavenly mystery is not profitably approached in rational terms. Our culture has for long elevated ordinary, ego-dominated states of consciousness to a position of prominence and desirability. The reality and usefulness of extraordinary, or altered states of consciousness has only recently been reintroduced to us by depth psychology and psychopharmacology. It is evident that in order to commune with an extraordinary kind of reality one needs to be in an extraordinary state of consciousness. The means of inducing such states are no doubt numerous and they may vary with the requirements of the times and of various traditions. Similarly, the utterance ensuing from such extraordinary states of consciousness also must be of an other than ordinary kind. Such an unusual modality of expression is the Hermetic hymn.

It is well known that the custom of singing hymns in connection with Christian religious services originated with the Gnostics, who like their spiritual relatives, the Hermeticists, used rhythmic religious poetry set to music in order to tell of their exalted experiences of Gnosis. The Syrian Gnostic teacher Bardaisan (born 155 C.E.) wrote a book containing 150 hymns which were used in the Christian community of Edessa for about 170 years. The orthodox Christian leader, St. Ephrem, then replaced the hymnal of Bardaisan with his own, which, however, was greatly inspired by its predecessor. The existence of hymns of a Gnostic and Hermetic origin bears testimony to the feeling-toned character of the experience of Gnosis and to the need for a special literary form to address and express this experience.

Mead and His Approach to Gnostic and Hermetic Wisdom

G. R. S. Mead, a highly intuitive and insightful scholar, whose literary activities fall into the latter part of the nineteenth century and the early part of the twentieth century must be regarded as a pioneer of the first order in the field of Gnostic and Hermetic studies. As the late poet and esoteric student Kenneth Rexroth accurately stated (in his introduction to the late 1950s University Books edition of Mead's *Fragments of a Faith Forgotten*), the only reason for Mead's continued neglect on the part of many academicians is the fact that he was a Theosophist. When in 1887, the redoubtable Madame Blavatsky settled in London, the young Mead joined the company of her close associates. In Blavatsky's circle he learned of the profound mysteries of the Gnostics and of the votaries of Hermes. Soon he became an indefatigable worker in his capacity of translator of Gnostic and Hermetic writings. In 1890–91 he began the publication in Blavatsky's journal of his translation of the great Gnostic work, *Pistis Sophia*, which became the first Gnostic codex to be available in a popular, yet accurate translation at that time and for many years to come. It was followed by various major works, and by an admirable series of small books, collectively entitled *Echoes from the Gnosis*, published over a period of several years by the Theosophical Publishing House in London. It was in this series of volumes, containing so many veritable gems of Gnostic and Hermetic origin, that *The Hymns of Hermes* was first published.

Over the years not all respected persons felt that Mead could not be valued because of his 'sinister' connections with Theosophy. According to a personal account given to the present writer by Jung's associate, the Gnostic scholar Gilles Quispel, C. G. Jung made a special journey to London in the last period of Mead's life to thank him for his pioneering work of translating and commenting on the Gnostic-Hermetic body of writings. What Jung valued in Mead was not only his outstanding scholarship and elegant use of the English language, but first and foremost his affinity toward the experience of Gnosis. Mead wrote about the ancient books of wisdom from the inside, as it were. Precisely because of his association with Blavatsky and her circle he justly felt himself as a spiritual relative of the seekers and finders of Gnosis long ago and far away. In this he was akin to C. G. Jung, who stated to Barbara Hannah that upon encountering the ancient Gnostics he was, at last, among old friends. Academic appreciation for such sympathies is still small indeed, as the Afterword to the third, revised edition of *The Nag Hammadi Library in English* clearly proves. A Richard Smith, managing editor of the work, accuses Blavatsky, Mead and C. G. Jung of appropriating Gnosticism for their purposes, without what he considers appropriate warrant. Unhappily, academic prejudice changes exceedingly slowly in our culture.

The story of modern Hermetic scholarship is a tortuous one. Until the latter part of the nineteenth century the Hermetic literature was most frequently regarded as a forgery perpetrated by Neoplatonists. By the 1850s and 1860s such scholars as Parthey, Artaud, Mènard and others began to question these ideas. In the early part of the twentieth century Reitzenstein published his translation of the *Poimandres* and proved the

Hermetica to be Hellenistic Egyptian spirituality. Mead squarely allied himself with the new view and was proven right. Perhaps the theosophical 'appropriators' of ancient traditions were not so badly informed after all!

G. R. S. Mead's greatest merit may be said to have been his ability to discern the inner, spiritual meaning of the Hermetic and Gnostic writings. His fervent spirit, stimulated by his theosophic orientation, entered the experiential core of these ancient records and perceived there a timeless message affirming the human potential for transformation and the ultimate insight into transcendence. For this, even more than for his scholarship, we owe G. R. S. Mead a debt of eternal gratitude.

Hermetic and Gnostic Renaissance

The influence of the Hermetic system on the best of Christian thought is beyond question. The perusal of the principal works of Clement of Alexandria shows many traces of influence by such teachings as we find in the Hermetica and among the Gnostics. Origen, in 230 C.E. taught in his *Principles* much that appears to come from the Hermetic wisdom, and his influence continued by way of his pupils, Gregory of Neo-Caesarea, Pamphilus, Dionysius of Alexandria, Basil the Great, Gregory of Nazianzene and many others. Nor was the influence of Hermeticism less upon numerous later Christian teachers, including the mysterious Dionysius the Areopagite, the sixth-century father of all Christian mystics. Acting through countless mystics of later times, the Hermetic core of Christian mysticism continued to shed its light and glory upon those inspired persons of the Christian faith who were desirous and capable of direct spiritual experience in preference to merely having faith in the experiences of apostolic men long ago and far away.

What motivated so many eminent Christian theologians and mystics to avail themselves of the Hermetic wisdom and to regard it in such a positive light, when at the same time so many of them were filled with abject horror regarding the extremely similar teachings of the Gnostics? The answer may be found in the fact that the Hermetic writings, being non-Christian in format and verbiage did not present any direct challenge to the dogmas of the Christian orthodoxy of various periods. The Gnostic teachings and myths, on the other hand, were too closely intertwined with Christian Biblical concepts and stories; they were uncomfortably close to the orthodox vision as it were, and thus radically disturbed the peace of mind of the Christian fathers. For very similar psychological reasons, many Jews and Christians today will rather immerse themselves in Hindu or Buddhist thought than investigate the

esoteric background of their faith, such as Kabbalah
and Gnostic Christianity.

By far the most influential development in connection with Hermeticism occurred in the fifteenth
century when, under the enlightened patronage of
the Medici princes, such scholars as Marsilio Ficino
and Pico della Mirandola undertook the translation
and dissemination of numerous important docu-
ments of the Hermetic tradition, which, for the
most part were recently transported from
Byzantium to Italy. It was not until the latter half
of the twentieth century that the full import of
these developments was recognized. In 1964 the
epochal work of the late Dame Frances Yates,
Giordano Bruno and the Hermetic Tradition was
published, to be followed by a number of outstanding works by the same author, who established
and proved the thesis that the Renaissance phe-
nomenon, both in Europe and in England was
primarily brought about by the spiritual stimulus
presented to the culture by the revived interest in
the Hermetic wisdom. Although the thrust of the
Hermetic revival of the Renaissance was blunted
by the Reformation and by the subsequent rise of
rationalism, its influence was never removed from
Western culture. A direct line may be drawn from
Bruno and the other leaders of the Hermetic Renaissance to Paracelsus, Boehme, the anonymous

writers of the Rosicrucian manifestoes, and later teachers. Some of these, like the illustrious Franz von Baader in Napoleon's time, endeavored to unite the Hermetic vision with the traditional teachings of Roman Catholicism, while others, including Saint-Martin, Swedenborg, Saint-Germain, Cagliostro and Mesmer exerted their efforts outside, and at times in opposition to, the Church. The Western esoteric tradition owes a great deal of its substance to the rediscovery of the Hermetic wisdom in the early Renaissance.

Today we may ask ourselves the question: Has the line of transmission extending from Greco-Egyptian wisdom come to an end? Has the Hermetic Renaissance finally run its course? In view of some comparatively recent developments we may answer: Perhaps not!

In December 1945, an Egyptian peasant and his brother, digging for fertilizer in the valley of Nag Hammadi in Egypt, discovered an entire library of Gnostic writings, originating in the early Christian centuries. It was the largest find of writings of this character ever made in history; its volume exceeded the total of all Gnostic books available up to this time. A group of new Ficinos and Pico della Mirandolas assembled and in 1977 presented the world with a complete one volume English translation, which generated a flood of interest in matters

Gnostic, which, now, a decade and a half after the publication, is still mounting. Not only the world of academic scholarship, but an ever-increasing general public has discovered the wisdom of the Gnostics, which in many ways seems to respond so fittingly to the great perplexities and agonies of our time. A Gnostic Renaissance may be at hand.

One may nourish the hope that the great translator of a hundred years ago, G. R. S. Mead, might in some way be aware of the present developments. More than anyone else, Mead was never wont to differentiate arbitrarily between Hermeticism and Gnosticism, but perceived them as two faces of the one body of Gnosis. In most of his writings, including the present volume, he freely and interchangeably quoted from both Gnostic and Hermetic sources. It is certain that he would welcome the present Gnostic Renaissance as a fitting continuation and culmination of the Hermetic renaissance of five hundred years ago. Weiser Books is to be congratulated on reprinting these Hymns in Mead's elegant translation. May they receive the reception which they so richly deserve!

—STEPHAN A. HOELLER

THE HYMNS OF HERMES

All textual references are to G. R. S. Mead's *Thrice-Greatest Hermes*, 3 vols. (London: Theosophical Publishing House, 1906).

THE SERVICE OF SONG

Clement of Alexandria tells us that the whole of the religious philosophy—that is, the wisdom, discipline and multifarious arts and sciences—of the Egyptian priesthood was contained in the Books of Hermes, that is of Thoth. These Books, he informs us further, were classified under forty-two heads and divided into a number of groups according to the various septs or divisions of the priests.

In describing a certain sacred ceremonial—a procession of priests in their various orders—Clement tells us that it was headed by a representative of the order of Singers, who were distinguished by appropriate symbols of music, some of which were apparently carried in the hands and others embroidered on the robes.

These Singers had to make themselves masters of, that is, learn by heart, two of the divisions of the Books of Hermes, namely, those which contained collections of Hymns in Honour of the Gods or God, and Encomia or Hymns in Praise of the Kings (iii, 222).

Many specimens of similar hymns in praise of the Gods are preserved to us in Egyptian inscriptions and papyri, and some of them are most noble outpourings of the soul in praise of the majesty and transcendency of the Supreme, in terms that may be not unfavorably compared with similar praisegiving in other great scriptures. But, alas! the hymnbooks of Thoth, to which Clement refers, are lost to us. He may, of course, have been mistaken in so definitely designating them, just as he was indubitably mistaken in thinking that they were collections of hymns composed by a single individual, Hermes.

The grandiose conception of Thoth as the inspirer of all sacred writings and the teacher of all religion and philosophy was Egyptian and not Greek; and it was but a sorry equivalent that the Greeks could find in their own pantheon when, in the change of God-names, they were forced to 'translate' "Thoth" by "Hermes."

Thoth, as the inspirer of all sacred writings and the president of all priestly discipline, was, as Iamblichus tells us, a name which was held by the Egyptians to be "common to all priests"—that is to say, every priest as priest was a Thoth, because he showed forth in his sacred office some characteristic or other of the Great Priest or Master Hierophant among the Gods whose earthy name was Thoth—

Tehuti.

Thoth was thus the Oversoul of all priests; and when some of the Greeks came to know better what the inner discipline of the true priestly mysteries connoted, they so felt the inadequacy of plain Hermes as a suitable equivalent for the Egyptian name which designated this great ideal, that they qualified 'Egyptian Hermes' with the honorific epithet 'Thrice-greatest.'

It is of the Hymns of this Thrice-greatest Hermes that I shall treat in the present small volume—hymns that were inspired by the still-living tradition of what was best in the wisdom of ancient Egypt, as 'philosophized' through minds trained in Greek thought, and set forth in the fair speech of golden-tongued Hellas.

But here again, unfortunately, we have no collection of such hymns preserved to us; and all we can do is to gather up the fragments that remain, scattered through the pages of the Trismegistic literature which have escaped the jealousy of an exclusive bibliolatry.

The main Gospel of the Trismegistic Gnosis is contained in a sacred sermon which bears in Greek the title "Poemandres." This may have been originally the Greek transliteration of an Egyptian name (ii, 50); but from the treatise itself it is manifest that it was understood by the Greek followers of this Gnosis to mean "The Shepherd of Men," or "Man-shepherd." This Shepherd was no man, but Divine Humanity or the Great Man or Mind, the inspirer of all spiritual initiations.

This majestic Reality or Essence of Certitude was conceived of as a limitless Presence, or Person, of Light and Life and Goodness, which enwrapped the contemplative mind of the pious worshipper of God or the Good, of the single-hearted lover of the Beautiful, and of the unwearied striver for the knowledge of the True.

And so, in His instruction to one who was striving to reach the grade of a true self-conscious Hermes, Poemandres declares:

> I, Mind, Myself am present with holy men and good, the pure and merciful, men who live piously.
>
> To such My Presence doth become an aid, and straightway they gain Gnosis of all things, and win the Father's love by their pure lives, and give Him thanks, invoking on Him blessings, and chanting hymns, intent on Him with ardent love (ii, 14).

And the same instruction is practically repeated in the sermon called "The Key," where we read:

But on the pious soul the Mind doth mount
and guide it to the Gnosis' Light. And such a
soul doth never tire in songs of praise to God
and pouring blessing on all men, and doing good
in word and deed to all, in imitation of its Sire
(ii, 155).

The sole conditions for reaching this consummation, so devoutly to be wished, are here laid down:

The good alone can know the Good; even as one of the invocations to Hermes as the Good Mind, preserved in the Greek Magic Papyri, phrases it:

Thee I invoke! Come unto me, O Good, Thou
altogether good, come to the good! (i, 86).

The pure alone can know the Pure; and by "Pure" I think Hermes sometimes meant far more than is generally connoted by the term. "Pure" is that which remains in itself, and is neither too much nor too little; it is the equilibrium, the balanced state, the mysterious something that reconciles all opposites, and is their simultaneous source and ending—the Divine Justice.

The merciful alone can know the Merciful, the source of the infinite variety of the Divine Love.

To such the Divine Presence becomes an aid; it is in the field of this 'Good Land' alone, in the self-cultivated soil of the spiritual nature—the good and the pure and merciful nature—of man, that the Divine Presence can sow the self-conscious seeds of the heavenly Gnosis, so that from this Virgin Womb of the Virtue may come to birth the true Man, the child of Freedom, or Right Will, or Good Will.

To others, to those who are still in ignorance of spiritual things, the Divine Presence is also an aid, but unknowingly; for being manifested for them in its reversed mode, by means of the constraints of Fate, the many consider it a hindrance, as indeed it is—a hindrance to their falling into greater ignorance and limitation. The soil must be cleared of tares and ploughed, before it can be sown.

But when man of his own freewill reverses his mode of life, and revolves with the motion of the heavenly spheres instead of spinning against them, the conscious contact with the Divine Presence which is thus effected, stirs the whole nature to respond; sunlight pours into the true heart of the man from all sides, and his heart answers; it wakes from the dead and begins to speak true words. The Great God gives speech to the heart in the Invisible, even as He does to the dead Osirified; and that unspoken speech is a continual praise-giving of right deeds. There is also a spoken speech, becoming articulate in human words in hymns of praise and thanks to God—the liturgy of a piety that answers to the Divine and is thus responsible.

Indeed this is the basis of all liturgy and cult, even in their crudest forms and reflections—in the dreams of men's sleeping hearts. But the Trismegistic writings are dealing with the self-conscious realization of true Gnostic Passion, where feeling has to be consciously transmuted into knowledge.

The singing of hymns on earth is the reflection of a heavenly mystery. Before the man can really sing in proper tune he must have harmonized his lower nature and transformed it into cosmos or fit order. Hitherto he has been singing out of tune, chaotically—howling, shrieking, crying, cursing, rather than singing articulately, and so offering 'reasonable oblations' to God.

The articulation of the 'members' of his true 'body' or 'heart' has not yet been completed or perfected; they are still, to use the language of the ancient Egyptian myth, scattered abroad, as it were, by his Typhonic passions; the limbs of his body of life are scattered in his body of death. The Isis of his spiritual nature is still weeping and mourning, gathering them together, awaiting the day of the New Dawn, when the last member, the organ of Gnosis, shall complete the *taxis*, or order, or band of his members, and the New Man shall arise from the dead.

It is only when these 'limbs' of his are harmonized and properly articulated that he has an instrument for cosmic music. It matters not whether the old myth tells us of the fourteen 'limbs' of the dead Osiris, or the later instruction speaks of the seven spheres of the creative Harmony that fashion forth the 'limbs' of every man, and views them as each energizing in two modes, according as the individual will of man goes with them or against them—it all refers to the same mystery. Man in limitation is two-fold, even as are his physical limbs; man in freedom as cosmicly configured is two in one in all things.

And therefore when this 'change of gnostic tendency' is wrought, there is a marvellous transmutation of the whole nature. He abandons his Typhonic passions, the energizings of the nature that has battled with God, in order that what the anonymous writer of that mystic masterpiece *The Dream of Ravan*, so finely calls the 'Divine Catastrophe' may be precipitated, and the Titan in him may be the more rapidly destroyed, or rather transmuted into the God.

For though these passions now seem to us to be of the 'Devil,' and though we look upon them as born of powers that fight against God, they are not really evil; they are the experiences in our nature of the natural energies of the Divine Harmony—that mysterious Engine of Fate, which is the seven-fold means of manifestation, according to our Trismegistic tradition. For the Divine Harmony is the creative instrument of the Divine Energy, that perpetually produces forms in substance for consciousness, and so gradually perfects a form that shall be capable of imaging forth the Perfect Man.

The natural energies that have been hitherto working through him unconsciously, in order that through form self-consciousness may come to birth, are, however, regarded by the neophyte, in the first stages of his gnostic birth, as inimical; they have woven for him garments that have brought experience, but which now seem rags that he would ain strip off, in order that he may put on new robes of power and majesty, and so exchange the sackcloth of the slave for the raiment of the King. Though the new garments are from the same yarn and woven by the energies of the same loom, the weaver is now laboring to change the texture and design; he is now joyfully learning gnosticly to follow the plan of the Great Weaver, and so cheerfully unravels the rags of his past imperfections to reweave them into 'fine linen' fit for King Osiris.

This gnostic change is in our treatise described

by the Great Mind teaching the little mind, as
following on the stripping off of the vices of the
soul, which are said to arise from the downward
mode of the energies of the seven spheres of the
Harmony of Fate. The subsequent beatification is
set forth in the following graphic declaration:

> And then, with all the energizing of the
> Harmony stript from him, he cometh to that
> nature which belongs unto the Eighth, and
> there with those that are hymneth the Father.
>
> They who are there welcome his coming
> there with joy; and he, made like to them that
> sojourn there, doth further hear the Powers
> who are above the nature that belongs unto the
> Eighth, singing their songs of praise to God in
> language of their own.
>
> And then they, in a band, go to the Father
> home; of their own selves they make surrender
> of themselves to Powers, and thus becoming
> Powers they are in God. This the good end for
> those who have gained Gnosis—to be made one
> with God (ii, 16).

This is the change of gnostic tendency that is
wrought in the nature of one who passes from the
stage of ordinary man, which Hermes characterizes as a "procession of Fate," to that true manhood

which leads finally to Godship.

The ancient Egyptians divided man into at least nine forms of manifestation, or modes of existence, or spheres of being, or by whatever phrase we choose to name these categories of his natures.

The words "clothed in his proper Power" refer, I believe, to one of these natures of man. Now the *sekhem* is generally translated "power," but we have no description of it whereby we may satisfactorily check the translation; and so I would suggest that the *khaibit*, though generally translated "shadow" (i, 89), is perhaps the mystery to which our text refers, for "in the teaching of Egypt, around the radiant being [perhaps the *ren* or name], which in its regenerate life could assimilate itself to the glory of the Godhead, was formed the *khaibit*, or luminous atmosphere, consisting of a series of ethereal envelopes, at once shading and diffusing its flaming lustre, as the earth's atmosphere shades and diffuses the solar rays" (i, 76).

This was typified by the linen swathings of the mummy, for "Thoth, the Divine Wisdom, wraps the spirit of the Justified a million times in a garment of fine linen," even as Jesus in a certain sacred act girt himself with a 'linen cloth' which Tertullian characterizes as the "proper garment of Osiris" (i, 71). And Plutarch tells us that linen was worn by the priests "on account of the colour which the flax in flower sends forth, resembling the ethereal radiance that surrounds the cosmos" (i, 265).

The same mystery is shown forth in the marvellous passage which describes the transfiguration of Jesus in the Gnostic gospel known as the *Pistis Sophia*, which is of almost pure Egyptian tradition. It is the mystic description of a wonderful metamorphosis or transformation that is wrought in the inner nature of the Master, who has ascended to clothe himself with the Robe of Glory, and who returns to the consciousness of his lower powers, or disciples, clad in his Robe of Power.

"They saw Jesus descending shining exceedingly; there was no measure to the light which surrounded him, for he shone more brightly than when he had ascended into the heavens, so that it is impossible for any in this world to describe the light in which he was. He shot forth rays shining exceedingly; his rays were without measure, nor were his rays of light equal together, but they were of every figure and type, some being more admirable than the others in infinite manner. And they were all pure light in every part at the same time.

"It was of three degrees, one surpassing the other in infinite manner. The second, which was in the midst, excelled the first which was below it, and the third, the most admirable of all, surpassed the two below it. The first glory was placed below all, like to the light which came upon Jesus before he ascended into the heavens, and was very regular as to its own light" (pp. 7, 8).

This triple glory, I believe, was the "body of light" of the nature of the eighth, ninth and tenth spheres of glory in the scale of the perfect ten. In our text the "clothed in his proper Power" must, I think, be referred to the powers of the seven spheres unified into one; the eighth, which was the vehicle of the pure mind, according to Platonic tradition, based originally, in all probablity, on Egyptian tradition. This 'vehicle' was 'atomic' and not 'molecular,' to use the terms of present-day science, simple and not compound, same and not other— "very regular as to its own light."

And so when this gnostic change is wrought in the man's inner nature there is an accompanying change effected in the substance of his very 'body,' and he begins to sing in harmony with the spheres; "with those that are he hymneth the Father."

He now knows the language of nature, and therewith sings praise continually in full consciousness of the joy of life. He sings the song of joy, and so singing hears the joyous songs of the Sons of God who form the first of the choirs invisible. They sing back to him and give him welcome; and what they sing the lover of such things may read in the same

Pistas Sophia (p. 17), in the Hymn of the Powers "Come unto Us"—when they welcome the returning exile on the Great Day of that name.

But this is not all; for higher still and higher, beyond and yet beyond, are other choirs of Powers of even greater transcendency who sing. As yet, however, the newly born cannot understand or bear their song, for they sing in a language of their own, there being many tongues of angels and archangels, of daimones and gods in their many grades.

But already the man has begun to realize the freedom of the cosmos; he has begun to feel himself a true cosmopolitan or world-citizen, and to thrill in harmony with the Powers. He experiences an ineffable union that removes all fear, and longs for the consummation of the final Sacred Marriage when he will perform the great sacrifice, and of himself make joyful surrender of all that he has been in separation, to become, by union with Those alone who truly are, all that has ever been and is and will be—and so one with God, the All and One.

It is thus evident that our Hymns of Hermes are in direct contact with a tradition which regarded the spiritual life as a perpetual service of song; and this is quite in keeping with the belief of the Egyptians that man was created for the sole purpose of worshipping the Gods and rendering them

pious service. The whole duty of man was thus
conceived of as an utterance of 'true words' or a
continual singing of a song of harmony of thought
and word and deed, whereby man grew like unto
the Gods, and so at last becoming a God was with
the Great God in the "Boat of the millions of
Years," or "Barque of the Æons," in other words,
was safe for eternity.

And now we will turn to the four hymns perserved
to us in Greek from the hymn-book of this truly
sacred liturgy.

The first is appended to the "Poemandres" treatise, and was evidently intended to give some idea
in human terms of the nature of the Praise-giving
of the Powers to which reference has just been
made. For, as we shall see later on, the less instructed
of the community fervently desired to have revealed
to them the words of this Song, thinking in their
ignorance that it was some hymn resembling those
of earth, and not yet understanding that it was the
heavenly type of all earth-praising, whether expressed by man or animal, by tree or stone.

The first part of our hymn consists of nine lines,
divided by their subjects into three groups, every
sentence beginning with "Holy art Thou!" It is
thus in the form of a three-fold "Holy, Holy,
Holy!"—and we may thus, for want of a proper
title, call it "A Triple Trisagion."

A TRIPLE TRISAGION

Holy art Thou, O God, the Universals' Father.

Holy art Thou, O God, Whose Will perfects itself by means of its own Powers.

Holy art Thou, O God, Who willest to be known and art known by Thine own.

Holy art Thou, Who didst by Word make to consist the things that are.

Holy art Thou, of Whom All-nature hath been made an Image.

Holy art Thou, Whose Form Nature hath never made.

Holy art Thou, more powerful than all power.

Holy art Thou, transcending all preeminence.

Holy art Thou, Thou better than all praise.

Accept my reason's offerings pure, from soul and heart for aye stretched up to Thee, O Thou unutterable, unspeakable, Whose Name naught but the Silence can express!

Give ear to me who pray that I may ne'er of Gnosis fail—Gnosis which is our common being's nature—and fill me with Thy Power, and with this Grace of Thine, that I may give the Light to those in ignorance of the Race, my Brethren and Thy Sons!

For this cause I believe, and I bear witness. I go to Life and Light. Blessed art Thou, O Father. Thy Man would holy be as Thou art holy, e'en as Thou gavest him Thy full authority to be.

"Holy art Thou, O God, the Universals' Father."

God is first praised as the Father of the Universals, that is of the Greatnesses of all things, the Æonic Immensities, or Supreme Mysteries that are plural yet one—the Subsistencies of the Divine Being in the state of pure Divinity.

"Holy art Thou, O God, Whose Will perfects itself by means of its own Powers."

God is next praised as the Power or Potency of all things; for Will is regarded by our Gnostics as the means by which the Deity reveals Himself unto Himself by the Great Act of perpetual Self-creation of Himself in Himself. "From Thee" are all things—when God is thought of as Divine Fatherhood; and "Through Thee" are all things—when God is regarded as Divine Motherhood. For this Will is the Divine Love which is the means of Self-perfection, the source of all consummation and satisfaction, of certitude and bliss. The Deity for ever initiates Himself into His own Mysteries.

"Holy art Thou, O God, Who willeth to be known and art known by Thine own."

The Will of God is Gnostic; He wills to be known. The Divine Purpose is consummated in Self-knowledge. God is knowable, but only by "His own," that is by the Divine Sonship, as Basilides, the Christian Gnostic, calls it, or by the Race of the Sons of God, as Philo and our Gnostics and others of the same period phrase it.

The Sonship is a Race, and not an individual, because they of the Sonship have ceased from separation and have made "surrender of themselves to Powers, and thus becoming Powers they are in God." They are one with another, no longer separated one from another and using divided senses and organs; for they constitute the Intelligible Word or Reason (Logos) which is also the Intelligible World (Kosmos) or Order of all things.

The next three praise-givings celebrate the same trinity of what, for lack of appropriate terms, we may call Being, Bliss and Intelligence, but now in another mode—the mode of manifestation or enformation in space and time and substance of the Sensible Universe, or Cosmos of forms and species.

The three *hypostases* or *hyparxes* or subsistences of this mode of the Divine self-manifestation are suggested by the terms Word, All-nature and Form. Word is the Vice-regent of Being, because it is this Word or Reason that established the being of all things, the that in them which causes them to be what they are, the essential reason of their being; All-nature is the ground or substance of their being, the all-receiver or Nurse, as Plato calls her, who nourishes them, the Giver of Bliss, the Ever-becoming which is the Image of Eternity; while Form is the impression of the Divine Intelligence, the source of all transformation and metamorphosis.

The final trisagion sings the praise of God's transcendency, declaring the powerlessness of human speech adequately to sing the praise of God.

Therefore is it said that the sole fit liturgy, or service of God, is to be found in the offerings of reason alone, the reason or *logos* which is the Divine principle in man, the image of the Image, or Divine Man, the Logos. It is the continual raising of the tension of the whole nature whereby the man is drawn ever closer and closer to God, in the rapt silence of ecstatic contemplation—when alone he goes to the Alone, as Plotinus says. The Name of God can be expressed by Silence alone, for, as we know from the remains of the Christianized Gnosis, this Silence, or Sigê, is the Spouse of God, and it is the Divine Spouse alone who can give full expression to the Divine Son, the Name or Logos of God.

The prayer is for Gnosis, for the realization of the state of Sonship, or the self-consciousness of the common being which the Son has with the Father. This is to be consummated by the fulfillment of the man's whole nature, by the completion of his insufficiency or imperfection (*hysterêma*), whereby he becomes the Fullness or Wholeness

(*Plêrôma*), the Æon or Eternity. This is to be achieved by the descent of the Great Power upon him, by the Blessing of God's Goodwill, that Charis or Grace or Love, which has been all along his Divine Mother, but which now becomes his Divine Spouse or Complement or Syzygy.

The prayer is not for self but for others, that so the man may become the means of illumination for those still in darkness, who as yet do not know of the Glad Tidings of the Divine Sonship, who are ignorant of the Race of Wisdom, but who nevertheless are, as are all men, brethren of the Christ and sons of God.

And so in this ecstasy of praise, the traveller, as he sings upon the Path of the Divine, feels within him the certitude that he is indeed on the Way of Return, his face set forward to the True Goal; his going to Light and Life, the eternal fatherhood and motherhood that are ever united in the Good, the One Desirable, or Divine Father-Mother, two in one and three in one.

Finally as God has been praised throughout in His nature of holiness, that is as most worshipful, meet to be adored, praiseworthy and the object of all wonder, so that which has proceeded from Him, His Man, or the Divine in man, now longs consciously to become of like nature with Him, according to the Purpose and Commandment of the

Father Who has destined him for this very end, and bestowed on him power over all things.

It is indeed a fair psalm—this Hymn of Hermes, that is, the praise-giving of some lover of this Gnosis who had, as he expresses it, "reached the Plain of Truth" (i, 19), or come into conscious contact with the reality of his own Divine nature, and so been made a Hermes indeed, capable of interpreting the inner meaning of religion, and of leading souls back from Death to Life—a true psychagogue. It matters little who wrote it; Greek or Syrian, it may have borne this name or that, it may have lived precisely from this year to that, or from some other to some other year, all this is of little consequence except for historians of the bodies of men. What concerns us here more nearly is the outpouring of a soul; we have here a man manifestly pouring forth from the fulness of his heart the profoundest experiences of his inmost life. He is telling us how it is possible for a man to learn to know God by first learning to know himself, and so unfold the flower of his spiritual nature and unwrap the swathings of the immemorial heart of him, that has been mummified and laid in the tomb so many ages of lives that have been living deaths.

And now we may pass to our next hymn. It is

found in a beautiful little treatise which bears as title the enunciation of its subject—"Though Unmanifest God is most Manifest"—and is a discourse of 'father' Hermes to 'son' Tat. The subject of this sermon is that mysterious manifestation of the Divine Energy which is now so well known by the Sanskrit term Mâyâ, so erroneously translated into English as "Illusion"—unless we venture to take this illusion in its root-meaning of Sport and Play; for in its highest sense Mâyâ is the Sport of the Creative Will, the World-Drama or God in activity.

The Greek equivalent of *mâyâ* is *phantasia*, which, for lack of a single term in English to represent it rightly, I have translated by "thinking-manifest." The Phantasy of God is thus the Power (Shakti in Sanskrit) of perpetual self-manifestation or self-imagining, and is the means whereby all 'This' comes into existence from the unmanifest 'That'; or as our treatise phrases it:

> He is Himself, both things that are and things that are not. The things that are He hath made manifest, he keepeth things that are not in Himself.
>
> He is the God beyond all name—He the unmanifest, he the most manifest; He whom the mind alone can contemplate, He visible

unto the eyes as well. He is the one of no body,
the one of many bodies, nay, rather, He of every
body.

Naught is there which He is not, for all are
He, and He is all (ii, 104).

He is both things that are 'here' in our present
consciousness, and all that are not in our consciousness, or rather memory—'there' in our eternal nature. He is both the Manifest and Hidden—
hidden in the manifest and manifest in the hidden,
manifest in all we have been and hidden in all we
shall be.

From the things that are not He maketh things
that are; and so He may be said to create out of
nothing—as far as we are concerned; indeed He
creates out of nothing but Himself.

He is both that which the mind alone can con-
template—that is the Intelligible Universe, or that
constituted in His Divine Being which the divided
senses cannot perceive—and also all that which
the senses, both physical and superphysical can
perceive—the whole Sensible Universe.

He is to be conceived simultaneously from a
monotheistic, polytheistic and pantheistic point
of view, and from many others—as many points of
view indeed, as the mind of man can conceive, not
to speak of an infinitude that he cannot ever imag-

ine. He is corporeality and incorporeality in perpetual union. He is in no body, for no body can contain Him, and yet is He in every body and every body is in Him. "Naught is there which He is not, for He is all."

It is indeed difficult to understand why so many in the West so greatly dread the very thought of allowing pantheistic ideas to enter into their conception of God. This fear is in reality over-daring or rash presumption, for they have the hardihood to dare to limit the Divine according to their own petty notions of what they would like God to be, and so they bitterly resent the disturbance of their self-complacency when it is pointed out that He will not fit the miserably narrow cross on which they would fain crucify Him.

What right have we, who in our ignorance are but puny creatures of a day, to exclude God from anyone or anything? But they will reply: It is not God who is excluded; it is we who exclude ourselves from God.

Indeed; try as we may, we cannot do so. This is the impossible, for we cannot exclude ourselves from ourselves. And who are we apart from God? Did we create ourselves? And if we did, then we are God, for self-creation is the prerogative of the Divine alone.

But the pious soul will still object that God is

good alone. Agreed, if you will; but what is Good? Is Good our good only, or the Good of all creatures? And if God is the Good of all creatures, then equally so must He be the Evil of all creatures; for the good of one creature is the evil of another, and the evil of one the good of another—and so the Balance is kept even. It is a limited view to say that God is good alone, and then to define this as meaning some special form of good that we imagine for ourselves, and not that which is really good for all; for it is good that there should be such apparent evil in the universe as pantheism, and that man's notions of apparent good should so far fall short of the reality. The wise man, or rather the man who is striving after Gnosis, is he who can see in the Good and Evil as conceived by man good in every evil, and evil or insufficiency in every good.

But if we say with Hermes that "All are He and He is all," we do not assert that we know what this really means, we only assert that we are in this declaration face to face with the ultimate mystery of all things before which we can only bow the head in reverent silence, for all words here fail.

And so the mystic who wrote these sentences continues his meditation with a magnificent hymn, expressive of the inability of the learner's mind rightly to sing God's praises, which, for lack of a better title, we may call "A Hymn to All-Father God."

A HYMN TO ALL-FATHER GOD

WHO, *then, may sing Thee praise of Thee, or
   praise to Thee?*

WHITHER, *again, am I to turn my eyes to sing
   Thy praise; above, below, within, without?*

*There is no way, no place is there about Thee,
   nor any other thing of things that are.*

*All are in Thee; all are from Thee; O Thou Who
   givest all and takest naught, for Thou hast
   all and naught is there Thou hast not.*

And WHEN, *O Father, shall I hymn Thee? For
none can seize Thy hour or time.*

For WHAT, *again, shall I sing hymn? For things
   that Thou hast made, or things Thou hast
   not? For things Thou hast made manifest, or
   things Thou hast concealed?*

HOW, *further, shall I hymn Thee? As being of
   myself? As having something of mine own?
   As being other?*

*For that Thou art whatever I may be; Thou art
   whatever I may do; Thou art whatever I may
   speak.*

*For Thou art all, and there is nothing else
   which Thou art not.*

*Thou art all that which doth exist, and Thou
   art what doth not exist,—Mind when Thou
   thinkest, and Father when Thou makest,*

[54]

*and God when Thou dost energize, and Good
and Maker of all things* (i, 105).

Who is capable of singing God's praises, when it
requires the whole universe of Being, and the
countless universes of all the beings that are, to
sing the praises of God in any truly adequate
manner? Who, then, what man, has the understanding wherewith to praise God fitly, when
though in his separated consciousness he knows
he knows not who he is, he yet begins to realize
that the "who he really is" must inevitably be God
and no other? In what manner can the Divine sing
praises of itself as of some other than itself, when
'I' and 'Thou' must essentially be one, and the
utterance of praise as of some other one seems to be
a departure from the blessed state of that Divine
intuition.

Is God again to be limited by space and spatial
considerations? Is there a 'whither' in respect to
God? Certainly there cannot be any special place
where the Divine may be said to be, for He is in all
places, and all places and spaces are in Him. He
cannot be said to be in the heart more than in any
other organ or limb of the body, for He is in all
things and all things are in Him. Equally so is there
no special direction in which the eyes of the mind

can turn, for He is to be seen in every direction of thought in which the mind can proceed; and if we say there are evil turnings of the mind, evil thoughts, he who has experienced this 'change of gnostic tendency' will reply that the only evil he now knows is not to be conscious that God is in all things, and that with the dawning of this true self-consciousness the right side of every thought presents itself with the wrong side in the joy of pure thinking.

The idea of the next praise-giving is perhaps somewhat difficult to follow, as it appears to be a contradiction in terms. But in these sublime heights of human thought all is seeming contradiction and paradox, because it is the state of reconciliation of all opposites.

It might be said that if God is He who gives all things, equally so must He be He who receives all things; but the antithesis can be equally well declared by the thought of all and nothing as by the idea of giving and receiving, for God manifestly takes nothing, in that He has no need of anything, seeing that He already has all things.

And if God cannot be limited by space, equally so is it impossible that He can be conditioned by time. Therefore the true Gnostic *Te Deum* cannot be sung at any one time only, but must be sung eternally; the man must transform himself into a perpetual song of praise in thought and word and deed.

Nor can the Deity be hymned for one thing, rather than for another, for all things are equally from God, and he who would make himself like unto God should have no preferences, but should view all things with equal eye, and embrace them all with equal love.

On account of what, again, as regards himself in distinction from the world, shall the Gnostic praise God? Shall he hymn the divine for the fact of his own self-existence, or because he is other than, presumably, the many who are not in Gnosis? The uselessness of all such distinctions becomes apparent in the doubt that the very asking of such questions awakens, and the devotee of Wisdom brushes them all aside in splendid outburst: "For that Thou art whatever I may be; Thou art whatever I may do; Thou art whatever I may speak." There is no separation in the reality of things. Whatever the man is in this ecstactic state, it is the Being of God in him; whatever the man does, it is the Working of God in him; whatever the man speaks, it is the Word of God in him.

Nay, more than this: to such a consciousness God is in very truth all things both manifest and hidden. God is Mind when we think of Him as thinking, devising and planning; God is Father when we conceive Him as willing and creating and bringing all things into existence; and God is Good when we regard Him as energizing or inworking or breathing in all things to give them Light and Life. He is the Good or End of all things, even as He is the Beginning or Maker of all.

Our next hymn is found in the marvellous initiation ritual which now bears the title "The Secret Sermon on the Mountain," with the sub-heading "Concerning Rebirth and the Promise of Silence," but which might very well be called "The Initiation of Tat."

This Rebirth or Regeneration was, and is, the mystery of the Spiritual Birth or Birth from Above, the object of the greater mysteries, even as in the lesser mysteries, the subject of the instructions was concerning the Birth from Below, the secret of genesis, or how a man comes into physical birth. The one was the birth or *genesis* into matter, the other the essential birth or *palingenesis*, the means of re-becoming a pure spiritual being.

It is the mystic rite of the 'laying on of hands,' the rite of invocation by Hermes, the hierophant or father on earth, whereby the Hands of Blessing of the Great Initiator, the Good Mind, are laid upon the head of Tat, the candidate, his son. These Hands of Blessing are no physical hands, but Powers, Rays of the spiritual Sun, even as they are

symbolized in the well-known Egyptian frescoes of
the Atem-cult. Each Ray is a Gnostic Power, the
light and virtue of which drive out the darkness of
the soul's vices and prepare the way for transform-
ing the fleshly body into the true ray-like or star-
like body of God—the *augoeides* or *astroeides*, to
which we referred under its Egyptian equivalent at
the beginning of this little volume.

This mystic rite of Gnostic initiation brings the
God in man to birth; he is at first, however, but a
baby God, who as yet neither hears nor sees, but
only feels. And so when the rite is duly ended, Tat
begs as a great privilege to be told the marvellous
Song of the Powers of which he has read in his
studies, and which his father, Hermes, is said to
have heard when he came to the Eighth Sphere or
Stage in his ascent of the Holy Mountain or Sacred
Stairs.

> I would, O father, hear the praise-giving with
> hymn which thou dost say thou heardest when
> thou wert at the Eight.

In answer to Tat's request Hermes replies that it
is quite true the Shepherd, the Divine Mind, at his
own still higher initiation into the first grade of
masterhood, foretold that he should hear this
Heaven-Song; and he commends Tat for hastening

to "strike his tent" now that he has been made pure. That is to say, the final rite of purification has now been operated in Tat, the powers of the cathartic or purifying virtues have descended upon him, so that he now has the power to 'strike his tent,' or free himself from the trammels of the body of vice, and so rise from the tomb which has hitherto imprisoned his 'daimonic soul,' as the Pythian Oracle says of Plotinus.

But, adds Hermes, it is not quite as Tat supposes. There is no one Song of the Powers written in human speech and kept secret; no manuscript, no oral tradition, of some physically uttered hymn.

> The Shepherd, Mind of all masterhood, hath not passed on to me more than hath been writ down, for full well did He know that I should of myself be able to learn all, and see all things.
>
> He left to me the making of fair things. Wherefore the Powers within me, e'en as they are in all, break into song.

The Song can be sung in many modes and many tongues, according to the inspiration of the illumined singer. The man who is reborn becomes a psalmist and a poet, for now is he tuned in harmony with the Great Harmony, and cannot do otherwise

than sing God's praises. He becomes a maker of
hymns and is no longer a repeater of the hymns of
others.

But Tat persists; his soul is filled with longing to
hear some echo of the Great Song. "Father, I wish
to hear; I long to know these things!"

And so Hermes is at last persuaded, and proceeds
to give him a model of such praise-giving which he
now can use in substitution for the prayers he has
previously employed, and which were more suited
to one in the state of faith.

Hermes bids Tat calm himself and so await in
reverent silence the hearing of the potent theurgic
outpouring of the whole nature of the man in praise
of God, which shall open a path throughout all
Nature straight to the Divine. This is no ordinary
hymn of praise but a theurgic operation or gnostic
act. Therefore, Hermes commands:

> Be still, my son! Hear the praise-giving that
> keeps the soul in tune, Hymn of Rebirth—a
> hymn I would not have thought fit so readily to
> tell, had'st thou not reached the end of all.

Not, of course, the end of all Gnosis, but the end
of the probationary path of purification and faith,
which is the beginning of the Gnosis. Such hymns

were taught only to those who had been made pure; not to those who were slaves of the world or even to them who were still struggling with their lower vices, but only to those who had got themselves ready and "made the thought in them a stranger to the world-illusion" (ii, 220).

"Wherefore," says Hermes, "this is not taught, but is kept hid in silence."

It is a hymn that must be used ceremonially at sunrise and sunset.

> Thus then, my son, stand in a place uncovered to the sky, facing the west, about the sinking of the setting sun, and make thy worship; so in like manner, too, when he doth rise, with face unto the east.

And for those who cannot perfect the rite on all planes, let them stand naked, with all the garments of false opinion stripped from them, naked in the midst of High Heaven's clear sphere, facing straight with the Spiritual Sun, or the Eye of Mind that illuminates the Great Sphere of our spiritual nature in stillness of the purified intelligence.

And so Hermes, before he sings what is called "The Secret Hymnody," once more utters the solemn injunction:

"Now, son, be still!"

THE SECRET HYMNODY

Let every nature of the world receive the
utterance of my hymn!

Open, thou Earth! Let every bolt of the Abyss
be drawn for me! Stir not, ye Trees!

I am about to hymn creation's Lord, both All
and One.

Ye Heavens open, and ye Winds stay still; and
let God's Deathless Sphere receive my word!

For I will sing the praise of Him who founded
all; who fixed the Earth, and hung up Heaven,
and gave command that Ocean should
afford sweet water to the Earth, to both those
parts that are inhabited, and those that are
not, for the support and use of every man;
who made the Fire to shine for gods and men
for every act.

Let us together all give praise to Him, sublime
above the Heavens, of every nature Lord!

'Tis He who is the Eye of Mind; may He accept
the praise of these my Powers!

Ye Powers that are within me, hymn the One
and All; sing with my Will, Powers all that
are within me!

O blessed Gnosis, by thee illumined, hymning
through thee the Light that mind alone can
see, I joy in Joy of Mind.

Sing with me praises, all ye Powers!

[63]

*Sing praise, my Self-control; sing thou through
me, my Righteousness, the praises of the
Righteous; sing thou, my Sharing-all, the
praises of the All; through me sing, Truth,
Truth's praises!*

*Sing thou, O Good, the Good! O Life and Light,
from us to you our praises flow!
Father, I give Thee thanks, to Thee Thou
Energy of all my Powers; I give Thee thanks,
O God, Thou Power of all my Energies.*

*Thy Reason sings through me Thy praises.
Take back through me the All into Thy
Reason—my reasonable oblation!*

*Thus cry the Powers in me. They sing Thy
praise, Thou All; they do Thy Will.*

FROM THEE, *Thy Will; To Thee, the All. Receive
from all their reasonable oblation. The All
that is in us, O Life, preserve; O Light, illu-
mine it; O God, inspirit it!*

*It is Thy Mind that plays the Shepherd to Thy
Word, O Thou Creator, Bestower of the Spirit
upon all.*

*For Thou art God; Thy Man thus cries to Thee,
through Fire, through Air, through Earth,
through Water, and through Spirit, through
Thy creatures.*

'Tis from Thy Æon I have found Praise-giving;

and in Thy Will, the object of my search,
have I found Rest (ii, 230–232).

We can see at once that this is no ordinary hymn, no hymn conceived in the mode of the psalms to which we have been used, but the gnostic outpouring of a man who has begun to realize the nature of his own spiritual dignity and proper place in the universe, based on the tradition of what is best in Egyptian theurgy, or that Divine energizing which sends forth words of command that all nature willingly obeys.

He is about to utter words 'that are true,' words that from the true go unto the True, without let or hindrance. Every nature will therefore receive such words and hand them on. All elements will hasten to serve the man who is serving God with the lawful liturgy of his whole nature.

The Earth in the midst, the Heaven above, the Abyss beneath, will open all the gates of their secret ways to let the true words of him who is 'true of word' pass onwards to the Deathless Sphere of the True God—that is, to the Æon itself wherein the True God dwells, not to some space of Heaven or of Earth or of the Abyss, but to that which transcends them, and is the source, preserver and end of all of them.

Not only the trees of the earth, but also the Trees of Paradise, the Divine Beings that dwell in Æonic Bliss, will rest in reverent silence as the potent praise of proper reverence passes to the end of all adorations.

The winds of earth will still themselves, and also the Winds of Heaven, the Intelligent Breaths in the inmost chambers of man's Greater Mind.

For the praise-giving is not poured forth to this or that daimon or god, but unto the Lord of All; and they, the Obedient Ones, whose life consists in praising God, cannot but rejoice that the Disobedient One should at last of his own freewill join in the unwearied liturgy of nature.

The hymn is in praise of the One and All, of the One Lord of all creation, who is both the One who creates and the All that is created. It is a hymn sung in harmony with the liturgy, or service of praise, of the four great primal natures, the Cosmic Elements of Earth and Air and Water and Fire—Father Heaven and Mother Earth, Father Fire and Mother Ocean. The man sings *with* them the glory of their common Lord, the Eye of Mind—that is, the Mind, the True Spiritual Sun, whose eyes are the countless suns in space. This True Sun is the True Light, the Light that mind alone can see; the little mind of man, now illumined by the Light of Gnosis, becomes of the nature of the Great Mind, and so a prismatic trinity of Good and Light and Life, through which the All-Brilliancy of the One and All shines forth in a septenary of Powers or Virtues.

These Powers are, with one exception, given in our hymnody in the exact classification in which they stand in the text of the mystic rite, namely: Gnosis, Joy, Self-control, Continence, Righteousness, Sharing-with-all, and Truth—which severally drive out Not-knowing, Sorrow, Intemperance, Desire, Unrighteousness, Avarice and Error. And with the coming of Truth the measure of the Good is filled full, for unto Truth is joined Good and Life and Light.

The nature of the persons of the latter trinity is still further revealed and the transmutablility of these hypostases, by praising God as the Energy of all Powers and the Power of all Energies, that is, as Light and Life again, Light the masculine energizer, and Life the feminine nourisher, the father-motherhood of God, the Good, the Logos or Reason of all things.

And so the gnostic psalmist at last resolves his praise-giving into the offering of a reasonable oblation—which, in final analysis, is the Song of the Logos; the Reason, the Son of God, the Alone-begotten, singing through the whole nature of the man and refunding the cosmos which is himself into the source of his Being. It is the consummation of the

Great Return; the Will of God is now the sole will of the man.

"*From Thee* Thy Will; *To Thee* the All."

That is, from Thee proceeds Thy Will; Thou art the Source of Thy Will, Thy Desire, Thy Love; and Thy Will is Thy Spouse, through whom are all things, the whole universe, Thy Alone-begotten, whose end also as well as beginning is Thyself, for He is Thyself eternally.

For as another mystic hymn of the period phrases it (i, 146): "*From Thee* is Father and *Through Thee* is Mother"—to which we may add "and *To Thee* is Son."

And so the hymn-singer continues with his 'reasonable oblation,' the offering of his true self, the *logos* within him, of his angel "that perpetually beholds the Face of the Father"—praying that his whole cosmos, the whole that there is of him, may be preserved or saved by Life the Mother, illumined or irradiated by Light the Father, and inspirited or inspired or spiritualized by the Great Breath of God that eternally and simultaneously outbreathes and inbreathes.

For the man is now no longer a single 'Letter' or a 'Procession of Fate,' but a true 'Name,' a free Man, a Word of God, a proper Cosmos, ordered in due and lawful harmony by conversion of self-will into a willing union with God's Will; and of that Word, or

God, or Angel, the Shepherd, or Feeder—He who gives the Divine nectar, or spiritual food, by which that Word is nourished—is the Great Mind, or Light, or Illuminator, the twin of the Great Soul, or Saving Life, the Inspirer and Preserver, both of which are bestowed upon us by God the Creator.

The man has now become a Man, a Word, a true Being of Reason, whose energy is expressed in living ideas that can be impressed upon the souls and minds of men, and lived out in a life of example; from an imperfect man he has become a perfect Cosmos or Order, or Harmony, and thus he can make his own purified natures sing together with the great elements and the quintessence of all of them, which is the Spirit or Breath of God, the Atman of Indian theosophy.

For having attained unto this true mode of breathing—breathing and thinking with the Great Life and Great Mind of things—the man is no longer a man but a Man, an Æon, an Eternity, and so rebecoming his own true Self he expresses his natural joy in songs of praise, and finds rest in the Great Peace, the Motherhood of God. He is born anew, a child Christ; and, as he grows in stature, towards full manhood, so will she, who has hitherto been his mother, refreshed with the eternal youth of the Gods, change from mother into spouse.

The remaining hymn that has been preserved to us in the extant Trismegistic literature is found at the end of "The Perfect Sermon," of which, unfortunately, the Greek original has been lost. We are dependent solely on an Old Latin version, which is frequently unsatisfactory.

This sermon is by far the longest of our extant Trismegistic *logoi*. The introduction informs us that Hermes and Asclepius and Tat and Ammon are gathered together in the *adytum* or holy place. There the three disciples reverently listen to their master, who delivers a long instruction of the Gnosis, with the purpose of perfecting them in the knowledge of spiritual things. The discourse is, therefore, rightly called "The Perfect Sermon," or "The Sermon of Initiation."

Asclepius, Tat and Ammon stand for three types of disciples of the Gnosis, three natures of man. Asclepius is the man of intellect, skilled in the knowledge of the schools, of the arts and sciences of the day. Tat is intuitional rather than intellectual; he is 'young' compared with Asclepius; nevertheless it is he who succeeds Hermes as teacher, when Hermes is taken to the Gods, for he has the spiritual nature more strongly developed than Asclepius, so that he can soar to greater heights of illumination. Ammon is the practical man of affairs, the king, the doer, not the scientist or the mystic.

It would, however, be a mistake to keep these types too clearly distinguished in our mind; for mystically all three are in each of us, and the true illumination of our three-fold nature depends upon the brotherly love of the three disciples—James, John and Peter—who must each complete each other, and subordinate themselves to one another, and vie with one another in love of their teacher, the purified mind, or Hermes, through whom alone the instruction of the Great Mind, the Shepherd, can as yet come to them.

And so we find the conditions of right contemplation dramatically set forth in the last sentence of the introduction of the sermon in the words:

> When Ammon, too, had come within the holy place, and when the sacred group of four was now complete with piety and with God's goodly Prescence—to them, sunk in fit silence reverently, their souls and minds pendent on Hermes' lips, thus Love Divine began to speak (ii, 309).

This Love Divine is that same Presence, the Highest Mind, or Shepherd of men, which illumines Hermes, or the higher mind within us, directly; but these immediate living words of power have to be passed on in human words to the three natures of our lower mind, the Asclepius and Tat and Ammon in us, who are the learners and hearers.

After the instruction is ended and they have come forth from the holy place, the narrative tells us that they turned their faces towards the setting sun, before uttering their hymn of praise.

That is to say mystically, the mind ceasing from contemplation, in which the outward energies have been caught up to the heights, or turned within, and stilled by the higher in the intercourse of Love that has been blessed with the Presence of the Divine, these energies, before betaking themselves to their appointed separate tasks, all unite in a hymn of praise, with their eyes still turned to the now apparently departing glory of the setting spiritual Sun.

Hereupon the knower of forms in us, the Asclepius who is wise in the sciences and arts, and ceremonies, proposes to Tat, in whispered words, that they suggest to their father Hermes, that they should say their prayer to God "with added incense and with unguents." This is the suggestion of the mind that still clings to outward forms, the ritualist. But Hermes recalls them to the gnostic nature of their spiritual cult.

> Whom when Thine greatest heard, he grew distressed and said:

"Nay, nay, Asclepius; speak more propitious words! For this is like to profanation of our sacred rites—when thou dost pray to God, to offer incense and the rest.

"For naught is there of which He stands in need, in that He is all things and all are in Him.

" But let us worship, pouring forth our thanks. For this is the best incense in God's sight— when thanks are given to Him by men" (ii, 388).

And so they begin their praise-giving, which for lack of a better title we may call "A Hymn of Grace for Gnosis."

A HYMN OF GRACE FOR GNOSIS

We give Thee grace, Thou highest and most
excellent! For by Thy Grace we have
received the so great Light of Thy own Gnosis.
O holy Name, fit Name to be adored, O Name
unique, by which God only must be blest
through worship of our Sire,—of Thee who
deignest to afford to all a Father's piety, and
care, and love, and whatsoever virtue is
more sweet than these, endowing us with
sense, and reason, and intelligence;—with
sense that we may feel Thee; with reason
that we may track Thee out from appear-
ances of things; with means of recognition

that we may joy in knowing Thee.
Saved by Thy Power divine, let us rejoice that
Thou hast shown Thyself to us in all Thy
Fullness. Let us rejoice that Thou hast
designed to consecrate us, still entombed in
bodies, to Eternity.
For this is the sole festival of praise worthy of
man—to know Thy Majesty.
We know Thee; yea, by the Single Sense of our
intelligence, we have perceived Thy Light
supreme,—O Thou True Life of life, O
Fecund Womb that giveth birth to every
nature!
We have known Thee, O Thou completely
filled with the Conception from Thyself
of Universal Nature!
We have known Thee, O Thou Eternal
Constancy!
For in the whole of this our prayer in worship of
Thy Good, this favour only of Thy Goodness
do we crave: that Thou wilt keep us constant
in our Love-of-knowing-Thee, and let us ne'er
be cut off from this kind of Life (ii, 389, 390).

We give Thee thanks, grace for Grace, goodwill for
Thy Goodwill. The Goodwill of God is, as we have
already learned, that "He willeth to be known," and
the goodwill of man is his "love of knowing God."

The Latin of the next sentence is very obscure, but judging by other passages and by the context, the unique effable Name of God is "Father." The worship of God as Father is true religion, piety and love, since these are the natural expressions of thanks to God, in that it is He who pours out on us the treasures of His piety and care (*religio* in Latin) and love, though indeed all of these words really fall short of expressing this Divine *efficacia*, or power of giving utter satisfaction, of God; for He alone gives without stint, in that He bestows His Fullness upon us.

He endows us with sense and reason and intelligence, the three means of knowing Him: with sense to feel God in all things; with reason to track out the manifestation of the Divine in all phenomena; and with intelligence, or spiritual intuition, which is the means of face to face recognition, when objective and subjective, and when object and subject blend and there is the complete joy and satisfaction of Self-knowledge.

The Power of God is the Will of God, the Goodwill, whereby He willeth to be known, that is to say, the Purpose of which is Gnosis; and this brings joy and rejoicing, for it is the manifestation of God to man in all His Fullness, that is to say, the manifestation of the Plêrôma, the Intelligible Cosmos, or God in the nature of His Alone-begotten Son.

The 'holy four' sing with joy in that they have been made holy, hallowed as priests of the Most High, while still in the tomb of the body; and so their very bodies have been consecrated as fit temples of the Son of God, the Æon or Eternity.

Therefore the sole festival of praise worthy of man in his divine nature, that is, in his true manhood or union with Great Mind—is to know God's Majesty or Greatness, that is, again, the Æon.

This Knowing, or Gnosis, is achieved by the Single Sense of the intelligence; not by sense alone, nor by mind alone, but by a means superior to both, in which the twain blend in Gnosis, and so become self-knowledge, or the Light of God, or the Over-mind of all things, and of the Life of God, or the Over-Soul of all things, which latter is graphically described as the "Fecund Womb that giveth birth to every nature."

This is the Gnosis of the Divine as the Plêrôma, or Fullness, which is replete with the Conception of universal nature from God Himself.

Finally, God is praised for being known as the Eternal Constancy, Stability, Duration, Unchangeableness, Sameness.

And so this beautiful gnostic thanksgiving or grace ends with the one prayer of those in Gnosis, namely, that He who is Eternal Constancy, or God in His energy of Æonic Sameness, will ever keep them constant in the Pure and Single Love, the Love of knowing God.

What noble hymns are these four, hymns worthy of all that is best in man, and all that is worthiest in the true worshipper of God! If only we had a psalter of such psalms, as doubtless once existed in this excellent community of servants of God and Gnostic liturgists! But alas! while the indifference of time has preserved for us so much of the classical writers that we could not unfrequently well spare, the jealousy of Providence has kept from us the major part of the most beautiful monuments of man's gnostic genius—perchance, however, because the world was not ready to appreciate them.

There is, therefore, nothing to do but to follow again the Way of the Hermeses of the past, and betake ourselves once more to "the making of fair things," for what man has once achieved he can again accomplish, and, if I am not mistaken in my augury, the times are again becoming ripe for such true poesy.

We have no more Hymns of Hermes wherewith to make glad the hearts of our readers—as we would fain hope they have gladdened them—but we will add another hymn of so like a nature that it might very well have been penned by a Hermes of the Trismegistic faith.

It is "A Song of Praise to the Æon," which is said to have been inscribed on a "secret tablet," by some unknown Brother of a forgotten Order, perhaps one of the Communities of the Æon—the Highest and Supercelestial One—which Philo of Byblos, in the second half of the first century of our era, tells us were in existence in Phœnicia in his day, and doubtless were also existing in Egypt (i, 403). The text is found in the Greek Magic Papyri.

A SONG OF PRAISE TO THE ÆON

Hail unto Thee, O Thou All-Comos of æthereal Spirit!

Hail unto Thee, O Spirit, who doth extend from Heaven to Earth, and from the Earth that's in the middle of the orb of Cosmos to the ends of the Abyss!

Hail unto Thee, O Spirit, who doth enter into me, who clingeth unto me or who doth part Thyself from me according to the Will of God in goodness of His heart!

Hail unto Thee, O Thou Beginning and Thou End of Nature naught can move!

Hail unto Thou, Thou Liturgy unweariable of Nature's Elements!

Hail unto Thee, O Thou Illumination of the Solar Beam that shines to serve the world!

Hail unto Thee, Thou Disk of the nightshining

Moon, that shines unequally!

*Hail, Ye Spirits all of the æthereal Statues of
the Gods!*

*Hail to You all, whom holy Brethren and holy
Sisters hail in giving of their praise!*

*O Spirit, Mighty One, most mighty circling
and incomprehensible Configuration of the
Cosmos, hail!—celestial, æthereal inter-
æthereal, water-like, earth-like, fire-like, air-
like, like unto light, to darkness like, shining
as do the Stars—moist, hot, cold Spirit!*

*I praise Thee, God of gods, who ever doth
restore the Cosmos, and who doth store the
Depth away upon its Throne of Settlement
no eye can see, who fixest Heaven and Earth
apart, and coverest the Heaven with Thy
golden everlasting wings, and makest firm
the Earth on everlasting Thrones!*

*O Thou who hangest up the Æther in the lofty
Height, and scatterest the Air with Thy self-
moving Blasts, who mak'st the Water eddy
round in circles!*

*O Thou who raisest up the fiery Whirlwind,
and makest thunder, lightning, rain, and
shakings of the earth, O God of Æons! Mighty
art Thou, Lord God, O Master of the All!*
(i, 408, 409).

The Æon is the Invisible Intelligible Cosmos, the All-Cosmos of Æthereal Spirit or Quintessence, as distinguished from the Sensible Cosmos of the four Great Elements, pure Fire and Air and Water and Earth, and not our mixed elements.

The reader has only to compare the opening and closing sentences of "The Secret Hymnody" with the first paragraph of our hymn to see that we are in precisely the same circle of ideas.

Heaven, Earth, and the Abyss, the three worlds, through which the Spirit, like Vishnu in the Purâna's, takes "three strides."

It is this Spirit, the Great Breath of Life, that is the out-breath and in-breath of man's manifold existences. When the Spirit breathes out he is born, from death into life, and also from life into death; for the life of the body is the death of the soul. And when the Spirit inbreathes he becomes dead, dead to things of the body, but alive to the things of the soul.

And all this is "according to the Will of God in goodness of His heart." For the Will of God is the Energy, or Effective Working, of God,—that which transcends all our human ideas of Love—dictated by the goodness of His heart, which ever wills the good of all beings, for the Heart of God is the Good Itself, the Æon.

The Æon is neither Beginning nor End, but both; for all the Spheres or Being which it energizes, end where they begin, and begin where they end—they dance in eternal revolution, for their "everlasting revelling-place" is in the Vortex of the Ceaseless Liturgy, or Service, of the Elements. The Æon is the Cause of the Magna Vorago, the Mighty Whirlpool of the Universe, for it is the Monad or Supreme Atom of all atoms and all combinations of atoms.

The Æon is the Illumination or Source of Light for all the Lights of Heaven, the Sun and Moon and all the rest of the "Æthereal Statues of the Gods"—the countless suns in space.

The Æon is Spirit, of Light and Life consisting, and so Father-Mother of all Spirits, whose true Bodies are the fiery spheres, the sidereal bodies—ray-like, star-like.

Therefore, the Brethren and Sisters of this community of gnostic servants of God rightly praise all the Gods, for these Gods are the true community of saints or holy ones in Heaven, even as the Brethren and Sisters are endeavoring to become saints on earth, holy as they are holy.

The Æon is the Great Paradigm or One Examplar of all things, the Eternal Configuration of the Cosmos and all cosmoi, in a septenary of three quintessential and four essential elements, which are completed by the all-color, Light, and no-color, Darkness, into a decad of which Spirit is the beginning and the end, existing in three modes—reminding us of the Trigunam, or three-fold nature of Prakriti or Nature in Indian theosophy—moist, hot, cold; black, red, white; Tamas, Rajas and Sattva.

The Great Work of the God of Gods is perpetually to restore the Cosmos, to refresh, to renew it, in its threefold nature of Height and Midst and Depth—the endoderm, mesoderm and ectoderm, as it were, of the cosmic germ-cell—over which the Spirit broods with its golden everlasting wings, as the Great Bird who perpetually hatches forth the Egg of the Universe.

And from this brooding there ever comes forth into being the perpetual cosmo-genesis of all things; and, seeing that all beings come forth from the Æon, each and all, in their cosmic nature, are Æons as well, so that the Æon is also God of Æons.

He is the God of millions of years, of millions of months, and millions of days—whether those time-periods be of the earth or of the universe—and so God of all existences, even as He is God of the Eternity of all things.

And here we must bring our little hymn-book to a close, in the hope that some may be found to sing in response to the Hymns of Heathen Hermes even in this twentieth-century of Christian grace; for perhaps, after all, Hermes and Christ are not in reality such strangers to each other as traditional theological prejudice would have us believe.